THE NATURE KIDS GUIDE TO

PEACOCKS

DAVID ANDERSON

LP Media Inc. Publishing
Text copyright © 2026 by LP Media Inc.
All rights reserved.

For information address LP Media Inc. Publishing,
30012 Variolite St NW, Princeton MN 55371
www.lpmedia.org

Publication Data

Peacocks
The Nature Kid's Guide to Peacocks — First edition.

Summary: "Learn all about Peacocks, the Nature Kid Way"
— Provided by publisher.

ISBN: 979-8-89818-134-5

[1. Peacocks – Non-Fiction] I. Title.

Title: The Nature Kid's Guide to Peacocks

CONTENTS

FOREST FLOORS

Wild peacocks live in forests that have lots of rain. These forests are called tropical or **monsoon** forests. The trees can grow over 100 feet tall!

Rustle! A peacock walks slowly through fallen leaves.

Peacocks live in wet forests and warm climates. They like places with tall trees and thick bushes. The forest floor gives them food and shelter.

These birds spend most of their day on the ground. They walk through leaves and grass. At night, they fly up into trees to sleep safely.

Peacocks need water nearby to survive. They often live close to streams or rivers. With food, shelter, and water, the forest provides everything they need to survive.

NATIVE HOMES

Squawk! A peacock calls out. Its bright feathers shine in the sun.

Wild peacocks come from Asia. Most live in India and Sri Lanka. They make their homes in the forests. They walk through grasslands too.

Peacocks have also spread to new places. People brought them to parks or farms. Some escaped and now live wild in their new homes.

Wild peacocks now live in the United States too. They live in Hawaii and in many southern states like Florida, Georgia, and Texas.

India loves peacocks! They made it their national bird in 1963!

BIG BIRDS

Thump! A peacock lands on the ground. This big bird makes quite an entrance!

Peacocks are large birds. Males can weigh up to 13 pounds and stand about 3 to 4 feet tall.

Their long tail feathers make them look even bigger. The tail can add 5 feet to their length!

Females are smaller than males. They weigh around 6 to 9 pounds. Both males and females have strong legs and big wings to carry their large bodies.

A peacock's wingspan can be around 5 feet wide. That helps them fly into tall trees.

FANCY FEATHERS

Swoosh! A peacock fans out its tail. Blue and green feathers shimmer.

Male peacocks have long, colorful tail feathers. They also have bright blue feathers on their necks and chests. This blue color comes from how light bounces off the feathers.

The long tail feathers have special spots. Each spot looks like an eye! These eye spots are called **ocelli**. They have rings of blue, green, and bronze.

Females have brown and gray feathers. This dull color helps them hide in bushes. But like males, they also have a crest of feathers on their heads.

A peacock's tail can have over 200 feathers. It takes three years to grow!

SHARP
SENSES

Screech! A peacock turns its head. It hears a sound far away.

Peacocks hear very well. They can hear sounds we cannot. Their ears hide under feathers. But they still work well.

Peacocks also see very well. They can spot danger far away. Their eyes see many colors too.

These senses help peacocks stay safe.

Peacocks can see in almost every direction. They do not need to move their heads!

TRICKY TAILS

Snap! A peacock spreads its tail wide. Bright eyes stare back.

Peacocks use their tails to scare predators. The eye spots on their feathers look like many eyes watching. This can confuse animals that want to attack.

When a peacock feels scared, it opens its tail fast. The sudden burst of color can startle a predator. This gives the peacock time to escape.

Peacocks also shake their tail feathers to make a rattling sound.

A peacock tail can have about 150 to 175 eye spots. That is a lot of eyes!

PICKY PECKERS

Peck! A peacock finds a bug. It gobbles it up fast.

Peacocks eat many different foods. They munch on seeds, grains, and berries. They also eat insects, worms, and small lizards.

Peacocks search for food on the ground. If you have ever seen a chicken eat, peacocks are almost the same. They use their beaks to dig in dirt and leaves. They eat whatever they can find.

These birds need lots of water too. Peacocks drink from streams and puddles every day.

Peacocks can even eat small snakes, frogs, and scorpions!

SCRATCH AND SNACK

A peacock can eat hundreds of ticks in one day. This helps keep forests healthy!

Scratch! A peacock digs in the dirt. It hunts for a tasty meal.

Peacocks scratch the ground to find food. They use their strong feet to move leaves and soil. This helps them uncover hidden treats.

These birds walk slowly while they hunt. They look down at the ground carefully. When they spot something tasty, they grab it with their beaks.

Peacocks often feed in the early morning. They also look for food in the late afternoon. During hot midday hours, they rest in the shade.

These birds often search for food in small groups. Together, they find insects and seeds hidden in the grass.

WATCH OUT

Stop! A peacock crouches low. It hears a leopard nearby.

Peacocks have many **predators**. Leopards, tigers, and wild dogs hunt them in the forest. These hunters move quietly through the trees.

Smaller predators are dangerous too. Mongooses and jungle cats sneak up on peacocks on the ground. Large snakes may eat peacock eggs or chicks.

Young peacocks face even more threats. Eagles and hawks swoop down from the sky. Peachicks must stay close to their mothers.

If a predator grabs a peacock's tail, the feathers pop right off!

FLY AWAY

Whoosh! A peacock flaps its wings hard. It flies up into a tree.

Peacocks can fly up to 80 feet high in a single burst. They flap their powerful wings to reach tree branches.

These birds fly up into tall trees every night. High branches keep them safe from predators below.

Peacocks prefer running to flying. Their long tails are heavy so flying is harder for peacocks than other birds.

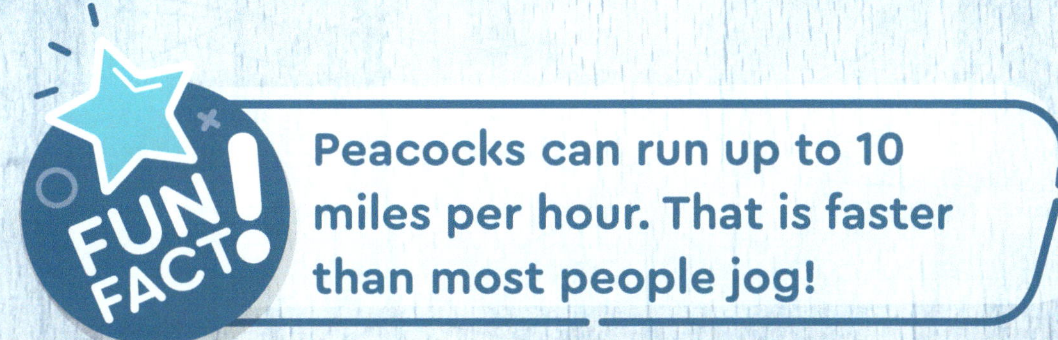

STRUT AND SPRINT

Stomp! A peacock struts across the path, its feet moving in quick steps.

Peacocks walk with high, careful steps. They lift their feet and place them down slowly. This helps them move through tall grass.

These birds can run fast when needed. They sprint up to 10 miles per hour to escape danger.

Peacocks spend more time standing than walking. But they still walk up to 2 miles each day.

A peacock's stride is about 16 inches long, with each step slow and steady as they search for food.

DAY BY DAY

DID YOU KNOW?

Peacocks spend about 12 hours each day just looking for food. That is half of their whole day!

Click! A peacock pecks at seeds as the morning sun warms its back.

Peacocks spend hours each day cleaning their feathers. They comb through every single feather with their beaks. A special oil gland near the tail keeps feathers shiny and waterproof.

Peacocks also take dust baths! They dig a shallow hole, lie down, and flap their wings. The dust soaks up extra oil and gets rid of tiny bugs in their feathers.

Afterward, peacocks spread their wings and sit in the warm sun. The heat helps the oil spread and makes the bright colors shine.

PARTY TIME

Chirp! A peacock pecks at the ground. His party is nearby.

Peacocks live in small groups. A group can have two to five birds. They stay together during the day.

Males often live alone or with other males. Females and their young form their own groups.

At night, these small groups come together. Many peacocks **roost** in the same trees.

A group of peacocks is called a party or a muster. Groups can have up to five birds.

SHOW OFF

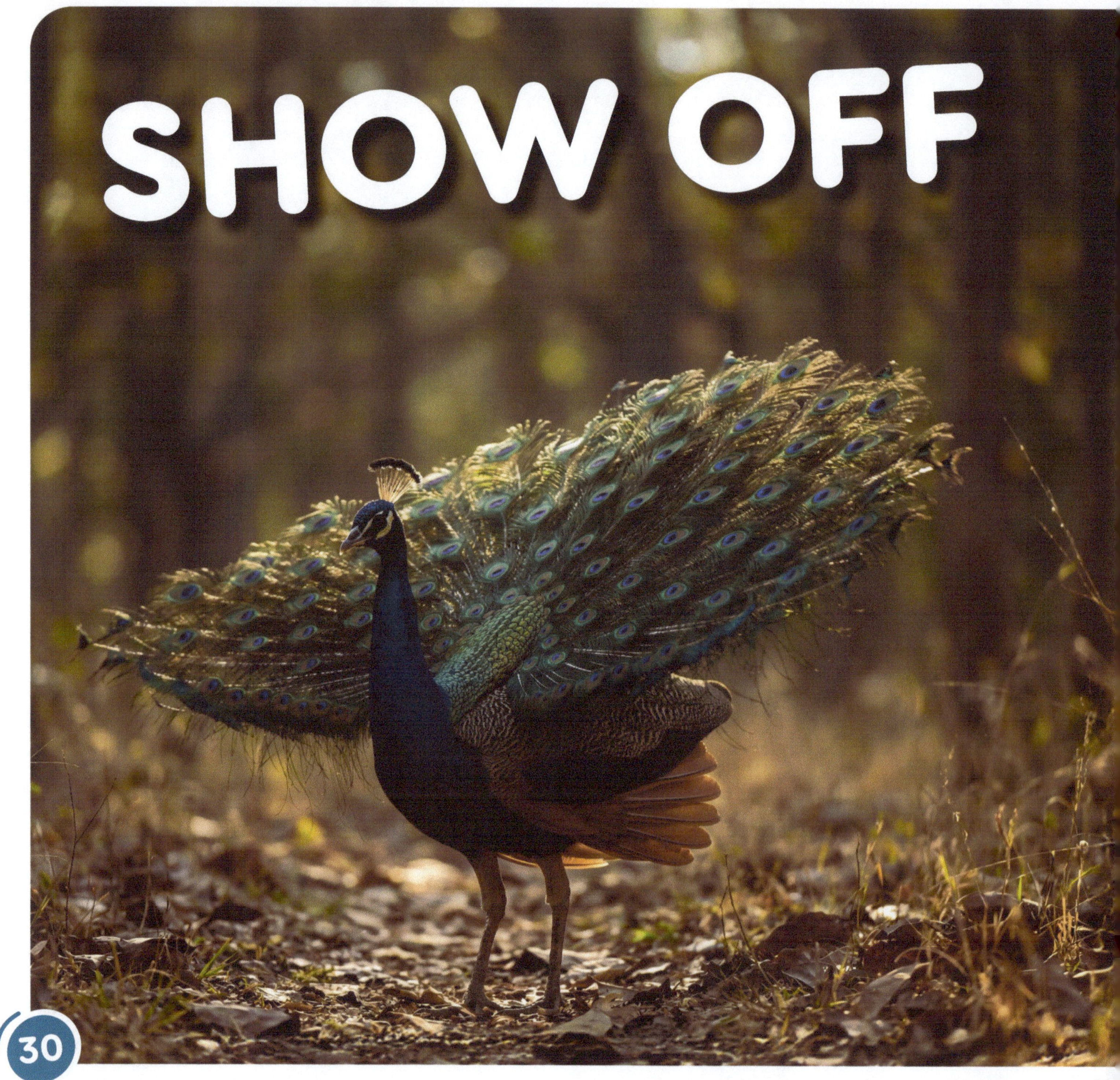

Rattle! A peacock shakes its tail. The feathers rattle loud.

Male peacocks show off their tails. They want to get a mate. They spread their feathers like a big fan. Then they shake them. This makes a rattling sound.

Females watch the males. They walk all around them. They look at the feathers from many sides.

Males do this many times each day. They do it in spring and summer. This is mating season.

A peacock's tail fan can spread over 5 feet wide. That is wider than most kids are tall!

PRECIOUS PEACHICKS

Peep! A young chick follows its mother through tall grass.

Baby peacocks are called **peachicks**. They hatch from eggs after about 28 days. These tiny chicks are covered in soft, fluffy down.

Newborn chicks can walk right away. They follow their mother within hours of hatching. She leads them to find food and water.

Peachicks can fly when they are about one week old. After a few weeks, their adult feathers start coming in. Young males do not grow their long tail feathers until they are about three years old.

FOLLOW MOM

Cluck! A mother peahen calls softly. Her chicks run to her side.

Mother peahens raise their chicks alone. Males do not help, so the mother does all the work.

Peahens keep their chicks warm at night. They tuck the babies under their wings. This keeps the little ones safe and cozy.

Mothers teach their chicks what to eat. They show them how to find bugs and seeds.

A mother peahen protects her chicks from danger. She makes loud calls to warn them. The chicks quickly hide in bushes.

Peahen mothers recognize each of their chicks by their unique calls.

SUPER SKILLS

Hiss! A peacock puffs up its neck. It looks much bigger now.

Peacocks have amazing skills. They can jump high into the air. Some can leap up to 8 feet off the ground!

Peacocks can puff up the feathers on their necks to make themselves look bigger. This trick works like a cat puffing up its fur. It helps scare away predators and warns other peacocks to stay back.

Peacocks can remember human faces for years! They also recognize other peacocks they have met before.

PEACOCK
PALS

Shake! A peacock shakes its feathers clean.

People have kept peacocks as pets and on farms for thousands of years. These birds need special care to stay healthy.

Peacocks need lots of space to roam. They like to walk and explore during the day.

Fresh water and food must be given daily. Peacocks eat grains, vegetables, and protein.

These birds also need shelter from rain and cold.

Peacocks can live for 20 years or more when people take good care of them.

GLOSSARY

ocelli
The eye-shaped spots on a peacock's tail feathers.

predators
Animals that hunt and eat other animals.

roost
To sleep or rest in a high place like a tree branch.

monsoon
A season with lots of heavy rain.

peachicks
Baby peacocks.